SILENCE

S I L E N C E

In the Age of Noise

Erling Kagge

Translated from the Norwegian by
B E C K Y L . C R O O K

VIKING
an imprint of
PENGUIN BOOKS

I

Whenever I am unable to walk, climb or sail away from the world, I have learned to shut it out.

Learning this took time. Only when I understood that I had a primal need for silence was I able to begin my search for it – and there, deep beneath a cacophony of traffic noise and thoughts, music and machinery, iPhones and snow ploughs, it lay in wait for me. Silence.

Not long ago, I tried convincing my three daughters that the world's secrets are hidden inside silence. We were sitting around the kitchen table eating Sunday dinner. Nowadays it is a rare occurrence for us to eat a meal together; so much is going on all the other days of the week. Sunday dinners have become the one time when we all remain seated and talk, face to face.

The girls looked at me sceptically. Surely silence is ... nothing? Even before I was able to explain the way in which silence can be a friend, and a luxury more valuable than any of the Louis Vuitton bags they so covet, their minds had been made up: silence is fine to have on hand when you're feeling sad. Beyond that, it's useless.

Sitting there at the dinner table, I suddenly remembered their curiosity as children. How they would wonder about what might be hiding behind a door. Their amazement as they stared at a light switch and asked me to 'open the light'.

Questions and answers, questions and answers. Wonder is the very engine of life. But my children are thirteen, sixteen and nineteen years old and wonder less and less; if they still wonder at anything, they quickly pull out their smartphones to find the answer. They are still curious, but their faces are not as childish, more adult, and their heads are now filled with more ambitions than questions. None of them had any interest in discussing the subject of silence, so, in order to invoke it, I told them about two friends of mine who had decided to climb Mount Everest.

Early one morning they left base camp to climb the southwest wall of the mountain. It was going well. Both reached the summit, but then came the storm. They soon realized they would not make it down alive. The first got hold of his pregnant wife via satellite phone. Together they decided on the name of the child that she was carrying. Then he quietly passed away just below the summit. My other friend was not able to contact anyone before he died. No one knows exactly what happened on the mountain in those hours. Thanks to the dry, cool climate 8,000 metres above sea level, they have both been freeze-dried. They lie there in silence, looking no different, more or less, to the way they were last time I saw them, twenty-two years ago.

For once there was silence around the table. One of our mobile phones pinged with an incoming message, but none of us thought to check our phones just then. Instead, we filled the silence with ourselves.

Not long afterwards, I was invited to give a lecture at St Andrew's University in Scotland. I was to choose the subject myself. I tended to talk about extreme journeys to the ends of the earth, but this time my thoughts turned homewards, to that Sunday supper with my family. So I settled on the topic of silence. I prepared myself well but was, as I often am, nervous beforehand. What if scattered thoughts about silence belonged only in the realm of Sunday dinners, and not in student forums? It was not that I expected to be booed for the eighteen minutes of my lecture, but I wanted the students to be interested in the subject I held so close to my heart.

I began the lecture with a minute of silence. You could have heard a pin drop. It was stock-still. For the next seventeen minutes I spoke about *the silence around us*, but I also talked about something that is even more important to me, *the silence within us*. The students remained quiet. Listening. It seemed as though they had been missing silence.

That same evening, I went out to a pub with a few of them. Inside the draughty entrance, each of us with a pint of beer, it was all more or less exactly the same as my student days at Cambridge. Kind, curious people, a humming atmosphere, interesting conversations. *What is silence? Where is it? Why is it more important now than ever?* were three questions they wanted answered.

That evening meant a lot to me, and not only for the good company. Thanks to the students I realized how little I understood. Back home I couldn't stop thinking about those three questions. They became an obsession.

What is silence? Where is it? Why is it more important now than ever?

Every evening I'd sit, puzzling over them. I began writing, thinking, and reading, more for myself than anyone else. By the end of my search I'd come up with thirty-three attempts at answering them.

II

1.

A lot of things in daily life boil down to *wonder*. It is one of the purest forms of joy that I can imagine. I enjoy the feeling. I often wonder, I do it almost everywhere: when travelling, reading, meeting people, when I sit down to write or whenever I feel my heart beat or see the sunrise. Wonder is one of the most powerful forces with which we are born. It is also one of our finest skills. Not only for an explorer like me: it holds just as much value for a father or for a publisher. I like it. Preferably without interruption.

Scientists can uncover truths. I would have liked to do that, but that path simply wasn't for me. Throughout my life my opinions on nearly everything have shifted. My sense of wonder is first and foremost something in and of itself, wonder for the sake of wonder. A small voyage of discovery. Though it can also be the seed that germinates, to bring forth new possibilities.

At other times, wonder is involuntary. It is not something that I choose, but rather I wonder because I simply cannot let it be. Something ugly from my past rears its head. A thought or an experience. It begins to gnaw at me and I can't stop thinking about what it might mean.

My cousin came to dinner one evening, and she gave me a poetry collection by a Norwegian author and playwright, Jon Fosse. After she left I lay on the bed leafing through the book. Just before turning off the light, these words surfaced: *there is a love no one remembers.* What did he mean by that? An invisible love that lies dormant? Could it be he was writing about silence? Good poetry reminds me of the great explorers. The right words are able to set my thoughts in motion, just like the explorers' accounts that I read when I was young. Before I fell asleep, I decided to write to Fosse the next morning, ask him about those seven words and try to draw water from his well.

'In a way it is the silence that speaks,' replied Fosse, six minutes after I had sent off my email. It almost seemed he had been waiting for my enquiry, yet that could hardly have been the case as he hadn't heard from me in years.

To speak is precisely what the silence should do. It *should* speak, and you should talk with it, in order to harness the potential that is present. 'Perhaps it's because silence goes together with wonder, but it also has a kind of majesty to it, yes, like an ocean, or like an endless snowy expanse,' he said. 'And whoever does not stand in wonder at this majesty fears it. And that is most likely why many are afraid of silence (and why there is music everywhere, *everywhere*).'

I recognize the fear that Fosse describes. A vague angst about something I can't quite put my finger on. Something which causes me all too easily to avoid being present in my own life. Instead, I busy myself with this or that, avoiding the silence, living through the new task at hand. I send text messages, put on some music, listen to the radio or allow my thoughts to flit about, rather than holding still and shutting out the world for a single moment.

I think the fear that Fosse expresses is a fear of getting to know ourselves better. There is a whiff of cowardice whenever I try to avoid that.

《 》

2.

Antarctica is the quietest place I've ever been. I walked alone to the South Pole, and in that whole vast monotone landscape there was no human noise apart from the sounds I made. Alone on the ice, far into that great white nothingness, I could both hear and feel the silence. (I had been forced by the company who owned the plane that flew me to the northern edge of Antarctica to bring a radio. The last thing I did in the plane was to leave the batteries in the rubbish bin.)

Everything seemed completely flat and white, mile after mile all the way to the horizon, as I headed southwards across the world's coldest continent. Underneath lie over 7 million cubic miles of ice, pressing down on the Earth's surface.

Eventually, in complete isolation, I began to notice that nothing was completely flat after all. The ice and snow formed small and large abstract shapes. The uniform whiteness was transformed into countless shades of white. A tinge of blue surfaced on the snow, somewhat reddish, greenish and slightly pink. The landscape seemed to be changing along the route; but I was wrong. My surroundings remained constant; I was the one who changed. On the twenty-second day I wrote in my journal: 'At home I only enjoy "big bites". Down here I am learning to value minuscule joys. The nuanced hues of the snow. The wind abating. Formations of clouds. Silence.'

As a child I was fascinated by the snail that was able to carry its own house wherever it went. During my Antarctic expedition, my admiration for the snail increased. I pulled all the food, gear and fuel I needed for the entire trip on a sledge and never opened my mouth to speak. I shut up. I had no radio contact, nor did I see a single living creature for fifty days. I did nothing but ski south each day. Even when I got angry, about a broken binding or because I nearly slipped into a crevasse, I did not curse. Lashing out brings you down and makes a bad mood worse. That's why I never swear on expeditions.

At home there's always a car passing, a telephone ringing, pinging or buzzing, someone talking, whispering or yelling. There are so many noises that we barely hear them all. Here it was different. Nature spoke to me in the guise of silence. The quieter I became, the more I heard.

Each time I stopped for a break, if the wind was not blowing I experienced a deafening silence. When there is no wind, even the snow looks silent. I became more and more attentive to the world of which I was a part. I was neither bored nor interrupted. I was alone with my own thoughts and ideas. The future was no longer relevant. I paid no attention to the past. I was present in my own life. *The world disappears when you go into it*, claimed the philosopher Martin Heidegger. And that is precisely what happened.

I'd become an extension of my surroundings. With no one to talk to, I began a conversation with nature. My thoughts were broadcast out over the plains towards the mountains, and other ideas were sent back.

In my journal southwards, I noted how easy it is to think that the continents that we cannot travel to, experience or see do not have much worth. One needs to have been to a place, to have photographed it and shared the photos in order for it to gain meaning. On the twenty-seventh day, I wrote: 'Antarctica is still distant and unknown for most people. As I walk along, I hope it will remain so. Not because I begrudge many people experiencing it, but because Antarctica has a mission as an unknown land.' I believe that we need places that have not been fully explored and normalized. There is still a continent that is mysterious, and practically untouched, 'that can be a state within one's fantasy'. This may be the greatest value of Antarctica for my three daughters and generations to come.

The secret to walking to the South Pole is to put one foot in front of the other, and to do this enough times. On a purely technical scale this is quite simple. Even a mouse can eat an elephant if it takes small enough bites. The challenge lies in the desire. The biggest challenge is to get up in the morning when the temperature is fifty degrees below freezing, in landscapes that mirror those of Roald Amundsen's and Robert Scott's times.

The next hardest challenge? To be at peace with yourself.

The silence adhered to me. Having no contact with the outside world, isolated and alone, I was forced to further ponder the thoughts that I already possessed. And, what's worse, my feelings. Antarctica is the world's largest desert, comprised of water, with more hours of sunshine than southern California. There's nowhere to hide. Those daily white lies and half-truths that we tell while we are back in civilization seem completely meaningless from a distance.

It may sound as though I meditated my way forward, but that's not how it was. At times the cold and wind gripped me like a pair of icy wire cutters. I froze until I wept. My nose, fingers and toes gradually turned white and the feeling in them disappeared. The pain arises when parts of your body become frostbitten, but then the pain abates. It returns again when they are thawed out. All the energy I could muster was consumed in trying to warm up again. It is more painful to thaw out frostbite than to freeze in the first place. Later the same day, when the warmth returned to my body, I regained energy to daydream.

Americans have built a base even at the South Pole. Scientists and maintenance-workers reside there for several months at a time, isolated from the outside world. One year there were ninety-nine residents who celebrated Christmas together at the base. Someone had smuggled in ninety-nine stones and handed out one apiece as Christmas gifts, keeping one for themselves. Nobody had seen stones for months. Some people hadn't seen stones for over a year. Nothing but ice, snow and man-made objects. Everyone sat gazing at and feeling their stone. Holding it in their hands, feeling its weight, without uttering a word.

《 》

3.

On my way towards the South Pole, I imagined the man in the moon looking down on the Earth. There wasn't a sound from our planet that was able to reach nearly 240,000 miles up to him, but he could see our planet and let his gaze wander far south. There, he saw a boy in a blue anorak trudging further and further in across the ice, only setting up his tent in the evenings. The next day he would emerge from the tent and the ritual was repeated. The man in the moon watched the boy head in the same direction, week after week. He must have thought the boy was nuts.

Late one afternoon, just before I was about to conclude my day's journey and pitch my tent, I peered up into the sky and imagined the man in the moon turning his gaze far north. Far below he could observe thousands, if not millions, of people leaving their tiny houses early in the day only to sit in traffic for a few minutes or an hour. As if in a silent movie. Then they arrive at large buildings, where they remain indoors for eight, ten or twelve hours seated in front

of a screen, before returning via the same traffic jam back to their tiny houses. At home, they eat dinner and watch the news on TV at the same time each night. Year after year.

The only difference over time would be that some of those people – perhaps the most ambitious of them – would move to a slightly larger house to spend their nights. As I released my ski-bindings that evening to pitch camp, I felt calmer and more content.

4.

At school I learned about sound waves. Sound is physical and can be measured in decibels, though I find it unsatisfying to measure sound with a number chart. Silence is more of an idea. A notion. The silence around us may contain a lot, but the most interesting kind of silence is the one that lies within. A silence which each of us must create. I no longer try to create absolute silence around me. The silence that I am after is the silence within.

I asked a world-class football player about *his* experience of noise down there on the pitch, in the midst of a crowded stadium, at the moment when he kicks the ball and it goes whizzing towards the goal. His reply was this: just after he's kicked the ball, he can't hear a single noise, even though the noise level has skyrocketed. He lets out a whoop. He is the first to know it's a goal. Yet the stadium continues to seem noiseless. His teammates are the next ones to understand that the ball has passed the goalposts, and he can see them cheering. Just after that, the fans realize it too, and then everyone is cheering loudly. The entire thing takes a second or two.

Of course, the noise level on the pitch has been at considerable decibel levels the whole time.

I believe it's possible for everyone to discover this silence within themselves. It is there all the time, even when we are surrounded by constant noise. Deep down in the ocean, below the waves and ripples, you can find your internal silence. Standing in the shower, letting the water wash over your head, sitting in front of a crackling fire, swimming across a forest lake or taking a walk over a field: all these can be experiences of perfect stillness too. I love that.

It's more difficult in Oslo. I work in the city, and at times I have to shape my own silence there. Sometimes there is so much noise that I turn up the music I'm listening to, not to create more of a disturbance, but in order to shut out other sounds. This seems to work if it's music that is already familiar to me and I'm not taken by surprise. You can even experience silence alongside an airport runway, if you really want to. A friend told me that the only time he can be certain of absolute quiet is when he is driving in his car.

The most important thing, as an old Norwegian saying goes, is *not how you are, but what you make of things*. For me, silence in nature is of the highest value. That's where I feel most at home. Still, if I hadn't been able to experience stillness amid city life, my longing for silence would be too great and I would have needed to return to nature more often.

The Arctic is an ocean surrounded by continents: a stark contrast to the Antarctic, which is a continent surrounded by oceans. When you are heading north on the Arctic ice, you are surrounded by constant noise. The Arctic Ocean is 3,000 metres deep and covered by ice. The ice is moved by the wind and the ocean currents. The enormous white masses rumble as they push against the elements of nature. Where the ice is thin, maybe only an inch, it sways and crackles as you walk.

*

In 1990, when the explorer Børge Ousland and I reached the North Pole, an American spy plane happened to fly overhead the day after we arrived. The pilots were probably just as surprised as we were to find someone else at the North Pole. As a gesture of kindness towards two famished polar explorers, they circled back and dropped a box of food before continuing on. After fifty-eight days in temperatures down to minus seventy degrees Fahrenheit, most of the fat and muscle mass had been burned off our bodies. In order to reach the pole, we had stretched our days from twenty-four to thirty hours, enabling us to walk for seventeen hours at a stretch. The cold and hunger had made it almost impossible to sleep at times. We opened the box from the spy plane. It was their lunch – sandwiches, juice, kippered herring – and we laid it all out on our sleeping mats and divided the food between us. I was about to devour my food when Børge suggested we shouldn't begin eating at once but rather pause for a moment. In silence. We should slowly count to ten internally and only then begin eating, he said. Show collective restraint.

Remind each other that satisfaction is also a matter of sacrifice. Waiting felt strange. But I have never felt as rich as I did in that moment of silence.

I don't knit, but when I watch someone who does, I think that they must have found some of the same inner peace that I discovered during my expeditions, even if their surroundings are not as quiet. It's the same when I read, play music, meditate, have sex, go skiing, do yoga or just sit quietly without any interruptions.

As a publisher, I have learned that it's possible to sell hundreds of thousands of books about knitting, brewing beer and stacking wood. A great many of us have a desire to return to something basic, authentic, and to find peace, to experience a small, quiet alternative to the din. There's something slow and sustainable about such pursuits, something meditative. The possibilities of being interrupted when you're brewing beer in your basement, or when knitting, are hopefully minimal, allowing you to relish the task at hand. Simply knowing that I am not going to be interrupted, and for once having an explanation for why I wish to be alone with my task, is a wonderful luxury.

This is not just a new trend, or a fad; it is a reflection of a profound human need. Knitting, brewing beer, felling trees; these are activities that all have something in common. You set yourself a goal and carry it out – not all at once, but over time. You use your hands or your body to create something. By moving yourself, you move your mind. I enjoy experiences where the satisfaction travels from the body to the head, rather than the other way around. The results that you achieve – firewood to warm you, a sweater you have poured yourself into – are not things that can simply be printed out. The fruit of your labour is a tangible product. A result that you and others can enjoy over a period of time.

5.

Sound, of course, is not *only* sound.

On a sailing trip in the spring of 1986, pushing towards Cape Horn off the coast of Chile in the south Pacific Ocean, I was reminded of this. Early one morning, while alone on watch between midnight and 4 a.m., I heard a sound that seemed like a long, deep breath just west of the boat. I had no idea what it could be. I turned ninety degrees in the direction of the sound and spotted a whale just off the starboard side. A mere calling distance away. I estimated that the creature was as long as our boat, about twenty metres. Judging from its length, I guessed that it was a fin whale, a cosmopolitan mammal on a lifelong hunt for crabs, krill and fish. Blue whales are about the same size, but as we have managed to nearly exterminate them, I figured the odds of the world's largest animal swimming alongside us were rather slim.

The sails were well trimmed, the boat was almost steering herself, and there was not much for me to do but watch that whale. Narrow, streamlined, a bit like a torpedo, with a greyish-black spine. The rule of thumb for large whales is that they weigh one ton per foot in length, so I guessed that the whale's weight was around sixty tons. He or she swam alongside the boat. For a few minutes we travelled the same course, my whale and I.

A few more times I heard that deep sound coming from the blowhole on its back, slowly in and out of the lungs, before the whale eventually vanished into the ocean. The world was not quite the same. I remained standing there, my hands on the wheel, listening and watching for that dark spine with the single fin, but I never saw my whale again.

When we came into port three days later, I heard the sound of a vacuum cleaner. That sound and the breathing of our whale were on nearly the same frequency. But whereas the one reminded me of normal, essential duties, something that I do as a chore to get rid of dust at home, the other sound is unusual, authentic, a primal force. I sometimes still hear that deep, majestic mode of expression; it's a source of enrichment for me even today.

《 》

6.

Silence can be boring. Everyone has experienced the ways in which silence can come across as exclusive, uncomfortable and at times even scary. At other times it is a sign of loneliness. Or sorrow. The silence that follows is heavy.

If there is something we don't want to talk about, we might just keep quiet. Girls who are around fifteen years old must be the unhappiest group of people on earth, so it was easy to understand what my daughters meant when they claimed that silence is important when they get upset. I do that myself – simply turn stony when my mood darkens. Whenever I observe a married couple avoiding each other with aggressive silence, I do my best to steer clear.

When I was little I often couldn't fall asleep. I lay there in my cot, tormented by silence. It was like having a nightmare and being awake at the same time, while my parents went about their activities in hushed tones. The silence felt like a sound, rumbling inside my head. From those nights, lying alone as I twisted and squirmed in my bed, I am unable to recall a single comforting thought.

However, silence can also be a friend. A comfort and a source of deeper riches. In *The Silence That Follows*, the poet Rolf Jacobsen wrote:

> *The silence that lives in the grass*
> *on the underside of each blade*
> *and in the blue space between the stones.*

The silence that rests like a young bird in your palms. It is easy to see oneself in Rolf Jacobsen's experience. Alone out on the ocean, you can hear the water; in the forest, a babbling brook or else branches swaying in the wind; on the mountain, tiny movements between stones and moss. These are times when silence is reassuring. I look for that within myself. From minute to minute. It might take place in the outdoors, but it could just as easily occur as I head to the office, when I take a moment to pause just before a meeting, or pull back from a conversation.

Shutting out the world is not about turning your back on your surroundings, but rather the opposite: it is seeing the world a bit more clearly, staying a course and trying to love your life.

Silence in itself is rich. It is exclusive and luxurious. A key to unlock new ways of thinking. I don't regard it as a renunciation or something spiritual, but rather as a practical resource for living a richer life. Or, to put it in more ordinary terms, as a deeper form of experiencing life than just turning on the TV to watch the news, again.

« »

7.

Contrary to what I believed when I was younger, the basic state of our brain is one of *chaos*.

The reason that it took me so long to understand this is that my days often pass on autopilot. I sleep, wake up, check my phone, shower, eat and head off to work. Here I respond to messages, attend meetings, read and converse. My own and others' expectations of how my day is supposed to unfold guide my hours up until the hour when I lie down again to sleep.

Whenever I fall out of this rut and sit quietly in a room alone, without any goal, without anything to look at, the chaos surfaces. It is difficult *only* to sit there. Multiple temptations surface. My brain, which functions so well on autopilot, is no longer helpful. It's not easy being idle when nothing else is going on, it is quiet and you are alone. I often choose to do anything else rather than to fill the silence with myself.

I have gradually come to realize that the source of many of my problems lies precisely in this struggle.

*

Of course, I am not the first person to have such thoughts. The philosopher and boredom theorist Blaise Pascal promoted this type of exploration as early as the 1600s: 'All of humanity's problems stem from man's inability to sit quietly in a room alone.' So a discomfort with being alone, holding one's tongue and simply *being* did not start with the advent of TV in the 1950s, with the coming of the internet in the '90s or with smartphones: it has always been a problem, and Pascal was probably the first to write about this feeling.

The constant impulse to turn to something else – TV series, gadgets, games – grows out of a need with which we are born, rather than being a cause. This disquiet that we feel has been with us since the beginning; it is our natural state. The present hurts, wrote Pascal. And our response is to look ceaselessly for fresh purposes that draw our attention outwards, away from ourselves.

Of course, such opportunities for interruption have increased dramatically over the last century, a trend that seems set to continue. We live in *the age of noise*. Silence is almost extinct.

One of Apple's founders, Steve Jobs, understood not only the benefits but also the dangers associated with using the technology that he helped to invent. Jobs limited his own children's access to Apple products. I have more faith in Steve Jobs as a responsible father than as a visionary marketing genius.

According to a much-referenced study, we humans are worse at concentrating than a goldfish. Humans today lose their concentration after eight seconds. In the year 2000 it was twelve seconds, while the goldfish averaged nine. I suspect that the research on goldfish is extremely limited and that the performance of these creatures should be taken with a pinch of salt. I mention this study for the conclusions it draws about humans: with each passing second, it seems increasingly difficult for us to focus on a single topic.

We find an echo of Pascal in a note by the writer David Foster Wallace, who is from the same generation as me:

Bliss – a second-by-second joy and gratitude at the gift of being alive, conscious – lies on the other side of crushing,

crushing boredom. Pay close attention to the most tedious thing you can find (Tax Returns, Televised Golf) and, in waves, a boredom like you've never known will wash over you and just about kill you.

But ride these waves out, he concluded, and it will feel like finally getting a drink of water after many days in the desert.

So Wallace's solution is to accept this state and then do something with it. It's about functioning well in an environment that shuts out everything that's vital and human: breathing without air. 'The key is the ability, whether innate or conditioned, to find the other side of the rote, the picayune, the meaningless, the repetitive, the pointlessly complex. To be, in a word, unborable.'

I stopped at that word: *unborable*.

Perhaps it should be the other way around – that it might be good for people to occasionally be a little bit bored? To refrain from plugging themselves in. To stop and wonder about what it is that we are actually doing.

I think that's what Wallace meant too. When he was a small boy, attending primary school, he shared his grand ambitions with his mother: 'I wanted to create a brilliant play, but it wouldn't start until all of the audience members except for one had left the theatre because they got so bored and quit the performance.'

I like that the only thing required here is endurance.

Ed Ruscha
Noise, 1963

8.

Research is currently under way on the validity of Pascal's assertion. In a joint study from the universities of Virginia and Harvard, scientists left individuals alone in a room for six to fifteen minutes without music, reading material, the chance to write or their smartphones. They were left solely to their own thoughts. The participants ranged from eighteen to seventy-seven years old and were drawn from a variety of social backgrounds, yet the results were the same regardless. Most felt discomfort. They reported that it was very difficult for them to concentrate during the minutes they spent alone, even though they were never interrupted.

A third of the participants who took the test at home have since admitted that they weren't even able to complete the assignment without breaking its rules, cutting short the minutes of sitting quietly.

It's kind of funny, imagining those lab rats sitting alone, cheating.

One group was permitted to read or listen to music

but was denied contact with other people. These participants reported higher satisfaction. Many of them also thought it was helpful to look out of a window.

The scientists then took the study one step further, in order to see whether the participants would rather do something unpleasant, such as receive an electrical shock, than sit alone in silence once again. Each participant had been subjected in advance to a similar electrical shock so they would know exactly how painful that option was. And it was painful. Nevertheless, nearly half of the subjects eventually pushed on the button to administer an electrical shock in order to reduce their silent time.

What was so striking, according to the researchers, was that being alone with one's own thoughts for fifteen minutes 'was apparently so aversive that it drove many participants to self-administer an electric shock that they had earlier said they would pay to avoid'. One of them pushed the electric shock button 190 times.

I don't think Pascal would have been surprised. On the contrary. He maintained that our constant flight from ourselves is a reality so brutal that we try to avoid thinking about it. We would rather think and feel anything else. He is right.

Would you then maintain that you and I are insane? Yes, I think we may be on our way to becoming stark raving lunatics.

Ed Ruscha
Talk About Space, 1963

9

Sometimes it makes sense to make life more difficult than necessary. To not just skip lightly over the lowest part of the fence. This is why I tried explaining to my children that I wanted to write about silence because it's more difficult to value silence than noise, and because it is important.

Silence is not first and foremost important because it is somehow better than noise, even if noise is often associated with negative events such as commotion, aggression and violence. Noise comes in the form of distracting sounds and images, and as one's own fleeting thoughts. We lose a bit of ourselves along the way. I am not only thinking of how exhausting it can be to process so many impressions. This is, of course, true, but there's more to it than that. Noise in the form of anticipating a screen or keyboard is addictive, and that is why we need silence.

The more we are inundated, the more we wish to be distracted. It should be the other way around, but often it isn't. You get into a *dopamine loop*. Dopamine is a chemical substance that transmits signals from one brain cell to another. In short, dopamine does what you desire, seek and crave. We don't know if we have received an email, message or other form of communication so we check and recheck our phones like a one-armed bandit in the attempt to achieve satisfaction. Dopamine is not programmed to release a feeling of fulfilment even if you've achieved what you sought and craved: so you are never satisfied. This means I continue to google, twenty minutes after I've found what I was initially searching for.

This is a banal predicament to find myself in. Still, I often find it easier to continue than to actually stop. I check websites that I just visited, even though I already know their content. And I relinquish a measure of control over my life in the process.

Biology has a natural explanation for my lack of common sense: we are not born to be satisfied. A different chemical in the brain, *opioid*, is supposed to create that feeling of happiness once you've achieved your goals. Unfortunately, dopamine is stronger than opioid, so even if you've attained all you ever dreamed of you will continue to do the same thing. Hence the *dopamine loop*. It is more fulfilling to anticipate and seek, to wander in circles, than simply to value and appreciate the fact that you have fulfilled your desires.

This is a form of noise that engenders anxiety and negative feelings. Most apps have one thing in common: no one uses them. Even successful apps like Twitter have eventually faced resistance. The founders are devastated that their own business idea is showing cracks and growth has slowed down. This is actually a good thing. The problem with achieving success with an app is that the service not only creates addiction – it fosters isolation as well. The basic business model of Twitter and other such social networks is to create a need for you to use the app, which the same app should then fill, but only temporarily. The owners live off your addiction. 'Gradually, these bonds cement into a habit as users turn to your product when experiencing certain internal triggers,' Nir Eyal wrote in his book *Hooked: How to Build Habit-Forming Products.* I share, therefore I am.

Some users get a good response when they post something on social media, while most sit waiting for anyone to care. And the more unpredictable this interaction is, the more the user is addicted. You don't want to miss out on anything. You don't gain happiness from such prolonged routines – rather, according to Eyal, you experience feelings of boredom, frustration, passivity and isolation.

For many people, it's about FOMO, the 'fear of missing out', or 'the fear of losing a special moment'. Eyal describes this as the brilliant driver for Instagram. And this last part is true: the app at the very least *is* nearly brilliant. But that moment which he is referring to is not necessarily something special. On the contrary. There aren't enough special moments, so we end up making do – repetitive and mundane moments are documented instead.

In the spring of 1984, I returned home to Norway after sailing in a thirty-five-foot boat to West Africa, and then across the Atlantic to the Caribbean and back again over the same ocean. My friends and I were gone for eight months. This was in the old days, before the expansion of the internet, so we hadn't received any news from Norway. The only exceptions were letters from girlfriends, friends and family that were sent poste restante to the harbours where we were expected. Back home again, I pored over newspapers and radio programmes the way I had habitually done before we'd set sail. I was surprised to realize that the news and debate programmes were broadcasting almost exactly the same content as when we had left the previous autumn. Politicians were mostly debating the same questions with one another. Even the arguments were the same.

When you've invested a lot of time in being accessible and keeping up with what's happening, it's easy to conclude that it all has a certain value, even if what you have done might not be that important. This is called *rationalization*. The *New York Review of Books* has labelled the battle between producers of apps 'the new opium wars', and the paper claims 'marketers have adopted addiction as an explicit commercial strategy'. The only difference is that the pushers aren't peddling a product that can be smoked in a pipe, but rather is ingested via sugar-coated apps.

In a way, silence is the opposite of all of this. It's about getting inside what you are doing. Experiencing rather than over-thinking. Allowing each moment to be big enough. Not living through other people and other things. Shutting out the world and fashioning your own silence whenever you run, cook food, have sex, study, chat, work, think of a new idea, read or dance.

10.

I am over fifty years old and have attended my fair share of sixtieth, seventieth and eightieth birthday parties. In case you are younger than me and have not yet celebrated so many birthdays of high, round figures, I can tell you that the most common remark heard at these parties is: 'All of those days that came and went – I didn't realize those were life.' It is cunningly formulated. The guests nod knowingly, smacking their lips. Yes, we fear death to varying degrees, but the fear of not having lived is even stronger. That fear increases towards the end of life, when you understand that it will soon be too late.

You are the one who is going to decide whether you will nod at the words or shake your head in disagreement. There's nothing criminal about sitting around a table decorated for a party and realizing that you've wasted much of your life. That you haven't been particularly present. That you've lived vicariously through others.

The unfortunate thing is to have wasted such a large

portion of the chance you had to live a richer life. That you avoided exploring your potential. Allowed yourself to be distracted. Never stopped, but were distracted by noise, expectations and images, instead of dwelling on what you were doing at this moment and what you might do differently. I don't mean to say that any of this is easy, but it may be worthwhile.

Instead of elaborating about the years that came and went with a champagne flute in hand, we should turn rather to the stoic Seneca on twenty-first birthdays: 'Life is long if you know how to use it.'

Even if we were to live for a thousand years, our lives would feel short if we threw away the time we actually had at our disposal. We *exist*, but few of us actually *live*, argued Seneca 2,000 years ago. 'Life is very short and anxious for those who forget the past, neglect the present, and fear the future. When they come to the end of it, the poor wretches realize too late that for all this time they have been preoccupied in doing nothing.'

I don't know how many times I've been told that most people in our part of the world don't experience material poverty, but rather a lack of time. It sounds like such a good thing to say, but it isn't quite correct. We *do* have enough time. Life is long, if we listen to ourselves often enough, and look up.

11.

One late night in December 2010, the urban explorer Steve Duncan and I climbed to the top of the Williamsburg Bridge, the bridge connecting Manhattan, Queens and Brooklyn. We were making our way through New York, from 242nd Street and Broadway in the Bronx, towards Harlem and further down Manhattan towards the Atlantic Ocean, via the city's mystical system of underground tunnels. Steve and I wanted to see New York in a way no one else has, from the inside out, and from the tops of bridges.

We made our ascent in the dark. Gazing out over Queens and Brooklyn all the way to Coney Island, we could detect the sun just below the horizon of the Atlantic. From the very tops of the bridge we watched the city slowly light up, even though the sun remained below the horizon. A few minutes later sunbeams hit where we stood, touched the upper floors of the skyscrapers below us, and then painstakingly began to warm up the city.

I heard nothing. Below me, the traffic thundered

past in four lanes, while the subway pounded rhythmically on its way in and out of the city centre. I was consumed by all that I saw and I shut out the noise. You cannot wait for it to get quiet. Not in New York, nor anywhere else. You must create your own silence.

On the opposite side of New York, where the sun never shines, my companion Steve and I discovered a different world. The architectural structure of the tunnels below the tarmac is a living organism that mirrors life above: tunnels are constructed, extended, courses altered, foundations set and buildings thrown up, and old systems of pipes are tied into the new as the underground terrain shifts – without anyone ever taking notice. This whole world is not only unknown to the city's inhabitants, but also to Google Earth. If Manhattan could be rotated 180 degrees, literally upside down, the island would be the man-made wilderness which we sludged through. A wilderness that has been formed solely for functionality, not aesthetics, but which nonetheless possesses its own beauty, a negative beauty – by virtue of all that is *not* present. There is no fresh air, the colours are only various hues of grey and brown, there is never any silence and we could hardly see what was up ahead. Yet it is precisely in the midst of all this that beauty exists, though it's not always easy to catch a glimpse of it.

The city never sleeps. New York's history has been shaped by the idea of earning a crust, and all of its noise ensues from this. The train, subway and water tunnels brim with ceaseless noise. Silence is absent even deep in the sewer system beneath Soho. In the far distance we could hear the thunder overhead. The tyres of cars rumbling across manhole covers followed by the long reverberation of metal. A subway running at full speed towards the next station in a nearby tunnel.

Over the five December days of our expedition we experienced the full cycle of civilization. Above ground: hectic Christmas shopping, lavish preparations, and restaurants crammed with hungry and thirsty guests.

Later that same afternoon, after we'd once again slipped below street level, the end product of civilization oozed past us in the form of excrement, forgetfulness, here and there a used condom or piece of trash. The sewer system in New York rarely uses pumps. Gravity is what moves the waste; everything flowed at the same speed, making a mild trickling noise around our legs.

At six o'clock in the morning, at the end of Greene Street, Steve and I sat relaxing on a stairway, literally soaked in shit after having attempted to cross the sewage system below Canal Street. Across from us, in a parking lot, I noticed a lone tree pushing upwards against the facade of a shabby old house. In the classic *Here is New York*, E. B. White describes existence in the city, while watching another tree in Manhattan, as: 'life under difficulties, growth against odds, sap-rise in the midst of concrete, and the steady reaching for the sun'. Why was that tree in front of us growing in that exact spot? How had the tree managed to survive the years with its leaves, buds, blooms, bark, moss, branches and tiny critters? One of the world's great mysteries is how organic beauty sprouts silently up from the ground. And in just that spot, on a couple of tarmac-free cubic inches of earth, it felt to me even more mysterious – a noiseless symbol for much of what we had set in motion. I had the subtle urge to go over and wrap my arms around that tree.

When I was young I read a story about women living in the Bronx and Harlem who worked in the exclusive shopping centres further south. They would arrive at work early so they could sneak into the book department. There they would sit in silence and read books they couldn't afford to buy, enjoying themselves until their shifts began. I liked that story, and imagined these women, sunk into deep sofas, each with her own book before opening hours. Maybe it was true. If it was, those women must have been happy in those brief moments, sitting and reading in peace.

As I stood atop the Williamsburg Bridge, I felt deep pleasure inside me, watching the sun rise from the

Atlantic Ocean to light up the city. If I were President, I would use my inaugural speech to challenge everyone to be thankful every time the sun rises and to show gratitude for all that it does for us.

But increasing along with the sunlight were the chances of the police soon spotting us. There's no way to get permission for undertaking such a climb, so we had no choice but to descend quickly. Steve, who was more experienced than I in these matters, reminded me that our expedition would really be at an end if we realized that traffic on the bridge had stopped and things suddenly got truly silent. In that case, it would mean the police had closed off the bridge and were on their way towards us.

《 》

12.

Everyone gets bored now and then. Obviously.

Boredom can be described as a lack of purpose. According to the Norwegian philosopher Lars Fr. H. Svendsen, boredom always gives the feeling of being held captive. When I was young, waiting for something to happen, I got bored to the point where it was almost painful. My mother told me it was healthy to be bored. Only now do I understand what she meant. Today I observe my children when they think nothing is happening: bored to tears, imprisoned in themselves, almost desperate. Like my mother, I feel it would be best if they could experience that more often.

I no longer get bored in the same way I once did. It's easier to find things to do as an adult. If you get bored you can simply talk with the person beside you on the Underground. I've tried it; it works. Though I don't have the desire to do it every morning.

If I've forgotten to bring along reading material and am sitting claustrophobically in seat 50F on an aeroplane without a film worth watching, or waiting for someone who doesn't show up to a meeting, I start to experience the feeling I had when I was little. What we are experiencing is *experiential poverty*.

Such poverty may not only be about a lack of experiences, where nothing is happening. An *abundance* of activities can also create a feeling of *experiential poverty*. And this last point is interesting. Things just get to be too much. The problem, according to Lars Fr. H. Svendsen, is that we carry on seeking 'increasingly more powerful experiences' instead of pausing to breathe deeply, shut out the world and use the time to experience ourselves. The idea that boredom can be avoided by constantly pursuing something new, being available around the clock, sending messages and clicking further, watching something you haven't yet seen, is naive.

The more you try to avoid boredom, the more bored you become.

Routine is like that too. I see my children grappling with the same issue. Busying oneself becomes a goal in and of itself, instead of allowing that same restlessness to lead you somewhere further.

Yet the differences between a lack of purpose that leads to boredom and the purpose that leads to happiness are not always easy to distinguish. The boundaries can be fluid at times. A pursuit that may seem like a waste of time on one given day, such as playing a game or watching a documentary, can provide a lovely, pleasure-filled pause on the next. Regardless, it is worthwhile reflecting on what brings purpose and joy. We should set a small goal to remember that next time.

13.

Today, as in earlier times, luxury is about both status and happiness, the type which very few people are permitted to enjoy. If King Louis XVI could be given back his head, which was detached during the revolution, his face would turn green with envy over your smartphone. Up until the moment he realized that nearly everyone owns one.

Luxury is an unessential product that is also scarce – or at least if enough people believe that there is a scarcity.

As the luxury branch grows – and luxury almost has become a public right – it has come to seem more commonplace and boring. The exclusivity of a Louis Vuitton bag diminishes if everyone has one. You can buy a new purse, but regardless of how great it is you will be overtaken by other purse-buyers who have even nicer purses than yours.

Some of the world's wealthiest people live, materially speaking, moderate lives, while others choose to bathe in luxury. My experience is that all those who bathe in luxury know one thing that others do not: luxury can only provide short-lived pleasure.

I believe silence is the new luxury. Silence is more exclusive and long-lasting than other luxuries. One of my daughters put this into words, to my delight, during her summer holiday: silence is the only need that those who are on the constant lookout for the latest luxury can never attain.

One difficulty with this is that something so straightforward and simple does not necessarily fit the category of luxury; silence is also an understated luxury. The *pursuit* of the luxury is first and foremost about attaining something by continuously adding to it. More, more. The dopamine in the heads of customers means they constantly crave more. Silence, on the other hand, is about *taking away*, subtracting something.

On top of that, silence is an experience that can be had for free. And it does not need to be replaced with the next season's luxury goods.

The chances of investing in silence – beyond peddling fancy noise-cancellation headphones, ads with people posed in desolate locations and hotels created for relaxation – are currently small. Business people are mostly just about business: what they want is more, not less.

Another form of luxury is to be *un*available. To turn your back on the daily din is a privilege. Letting others take over tasks in your absence. The decision not to reply to text messages or pick up when the phone rings. Expectations from colleagues, business connections and family that are not that important to you are handed over to someone else, or ignored altogether. You have fought your way into a position where you couldn't care less if someone wants to contact you.

Noise is also connected to class divisions. Noises made by anyone other than the person being disturbed by them, *secondary sounds*, set the foundation for great disparities in society. People in the lower classes are usually forced to tolerate more noise in the workplace than those in the upper classes, and their homes are poorly insulated against their neighbours' noise. Wealthy people live in places with less noise and better air, their cars run more quietly, as do their washers and dryers. They have more free time and eat cleaner, healthier food. Silence has become part of the disparity that gives some few people the opportunity to have a longer, healthier, richer life than most others.

There are very few people who are able to avoid noise altogether. We learn to live with it because we think that we must, but noise is and remains a disturbing element that reduces our quality of life. Not only for people, but for animals as well. I love waking up to birdsong, and there have been studies on how birds react to increasing noise levels in urban areas. The conclusion is that the songs of the birds have changed. Lower tones have disappeared and been replaced by higher noises that are able to compete with human noise. One consequence of this adapted birdsong is that it has become more difficult for birds to attract a mate. Thus fewer eggs are laid. The development has been rapid, and researchers don't know yet whether this is an evolutionary shift. The cause is closer to home: birds inhabiting urban areas are more agitated by the soundscape. Birds and people are different, but I nonetheless recognize the uncertainty they exhibit. Silence is a luxury for every living creature.

14.

One summer I flew eighteen hours from Oslo to Sri Lanka in order to relax, eat healthily and practise yoga in lush surroundings. It was fabulous. At the same time, it felt strange to travel halfway around the globe to disconnect.

Some people fabricate favourable conditions for silence by constructing soundproof rooms or homes. In Jutland, Denmark, they have built a soundproofed hall of silence with double doors that are thirty centimetres apart. Dozens of people gather here regularly. They sit cross-legged on their individual pillows for fifty minutes. The only break in the silence is a few coughs and other sounds that the participants can't quite suppress. The goal is for them to be reminded, over time, that life is about deep love between people, and to enable them to practise a common empathy.

Centres for silence are a growing industry, and they are popping up everywhere. Located at the end of

Sunset Boulevard in LA, the Lake Shrine Temple promises 'silence of solitude'. I went there following a four-day walk through the entire city, from the gang area on the east side heading west towards the ocean. Everyone drives in LA, and we wanted to see the city from the sidewalk. As we walked, we were stopped by police officers suspicious of us because we weren't driving. The policemen claimed that only robbers, junkies and mentally unstable people would walk around the city. Following long, dusty stretches on the sidewalk, it was not hard to find peace at the temple, with its lake, carp, flowers and silence. Afterwards we took a dip in the Pacific, five minutes away, and it was just as quiet there. When I am out trekking across the Norwegian wilderness or in the Himalayas, I also come across facilities where visitors may experience silence. If you venture a bit further away from them, you'll find it is quieter still.

Fabricating conditions for silence is a fine undertaking, but it can be a bit tedious to drive a car in order to arrive at a place where you can calm down, do some yoga, go for a walk, or take an aeroplane in order to disconnect at a retreat. The best things in life are sometimes free. The silence I have in mind may be found wherever you are, if you pay attention, inside your mind, and is without cost. You don't have to go to Sri Lanka: you can experience it in your bathtub.

I discover silence when I stay five extra minutes in bed at home (now the kids are old enough to get up by themselves). Or on my way into work in the morning. I have the choice of driving through traffic for twelve minutes, spending a quarter of an hour on the Underground, or walking for thirty minutes. I'm able to disconnect in the car, but I must remain aware of traffic, and I switch the radio on too. The subway is packed and when you get to your destination everyone pushes to get out all at once. So, if time allows, I choose to walk. Everything that I am unable to see from the car window or subway tunnel becomes a part of my everyday life. Faces that I can study as I pass, attire that changes with the weather, the windows of cafés and shops, variations in the tarmac and cobbles that someone has laboriously laid.

Walking to work is no grand experience, yet there is some small value to it. It takes me no longer than thirty minutes to walk between the two addresses where I most often find myself, and in that time I have managed to shut out the world.

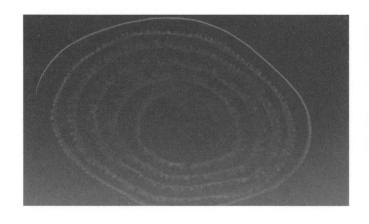

Doug Aitken
Modern Soul, 2016

15.

Silence is about rediscovering, through pausing, the things that bring us joy.

My children hardly pause any more. They are always accessible, and almost always busy. 'Everyone is the other, no one is themselves,' wrote Martin Heidegger. The three of them tend to sit in front of a screen – whether alone or together with others. I do it too. Become engulfed in my smartphone, enslave myself to my own tablet – as a consumer and at times as a producer. I am constantly interrupted, interruptions engendered by other interruptions. I rummage around in a world that has little to do with me. Attempt to be effective until I realize I won't get any further regardless of how effective I've become. It feels like trying to find your way through fog on a mountain, without a compass at hand, and ending up walking around in circles. The goal is to be busy and effective, nothing else.

It is easy to assume that the essence of technology is technology itself, but that is wrong. The essence is you and me. It's about how we are altered by the technology we employ, what we hope to learn, our relationship with nature, those we love, the time we spend, the energy that is consumed, and how much freedom we relinquish to technology. Yes, it's true what many say, that distances are eclipsed by technology, but that is a banal fact. The central issue is rather, as Heidegger pointed out, that: 'nearness remains outstanding'. In order to achieve nearness, we must, according to the derided philosopher, relate to the truth, not to technology. Having tried my hand at internet dating, I am inclined to agree with Heidegger.

(Of course, Heidegger could not have predicted the possibilities offered by current technology. He was thinking about cars of fifty horsepower, film projectors and punch-card machines, which were all the rage. But he had an inkling of what might come.)

We are going to give up our own freedom in our eagerness to use new technology, Heidegger claimed. To shift from being free people to becoming resources. The thought is even more fitting now than when he first expressed it. We will not become a resource for one another, unfortunately, but for something less appealing. A resource for organizations such as Apple, Facebook, Instagram, Google, Snapchat and governments, who are trying to map us all out, with our voluntary assistance, in order to use or sell the information. It smacks of exploitation.

The question that Humpty Dumpty poses to Alice remains: 'which is to be master – that's all'. You, or someone you don't know?

Humans are social creatures. Being accessible can be a good thing. We are unable to function alone. Yet it's important to be able to turn off your phone, sit down, not say anything, shut your eyes, breathe deeply a couple of times and attempt to think about something other than what you are normally thinking about.

The alternative is to not think anything at all. You may call this meditation, yoga, mindfulness or merely common sense. It can be good. I take pleasure in meditating and practising yoga. I've also taken up the cousin to this practice – hypnosis – and hypnotize myself for twenty minutes in order to disconnect.

That also works well. I lie there hovering a couple of centimetres above my bed each afternoon.

I find myself thinking about how silence can be experienced without the use of techniques. The threshold for finding silence and balance can in fact be lowered. You don't need a course in silence or relaxation to be able simply to pause. Silence can be anywhere, anytime – it's just in front of your nose. I create it for myself as I walk up the stairs, prepare food or merely focus on my breathing. Sure, we are all part of the same continent, but the potential wealth of being an island for yourself is something you carry around with you all the time.

16.

How should we live? That's one of the biggest of the
big questions. In the old days, great and not-so-great
philosophers made attempts to find the answer. The
result was extensive theories and loads of reading
material. Most philosophers nowadays are geared
towards politics, language and analytics. Few
philosophers focus on silence and what it can do for
you and me. Several philosophers have remarked to
me, in much the same vein as my children's comments
around the dinner table, that silence is nothing and
therefore uninteresting. That's a pity. On the other
hand, few philosophers are able to bake a cake – so
many of them are far removed from both the small
and big challenges of practical, everyday life.

In the first year of philosophy studies you are taught
that from nothing comes nothing. *Ex nihilo, nihil fit.*
The proposition is as apt as it is ancient – the
philosopher Parmenides claimed that it was impossible
to speak about that which does not exist, and with
that he broke his own proposition, to the amusement

of many – but I think that, in this case, the conclusion is based on a tiny misunderstanding.

After all, silence is not nothing. It is better to say that from something comes something.

For thousands of years, individuals who lived in close quarters with no one but themselves around – monks on mountaintops, hermits, sailors, shepherds and explorers on their voyage home – have been convinced that the answer to life's mysteries can be found in silence. That is the point. You sail out across the sea, but it's when you make your return that you may discover what you have been seeking is in fact inside yourself.

The same claim has been repeated for such a long time, so there's probably a good reason to take it seriously. Jesus and Buddha ventured into silence in order to understand how they should live. Jesus to the wilderness and Buddha to the mountain and river. In silence, Jesus prepared himself for God. The river taught Buddha to hear, to listen with a still heart, and with a waiting, open mind.

In some religions the gods appear as a thunder crack or a storm. In the Bible, God is often the silence. In the Book of Kings, we are told of the way in which God reveals himself to Elijah. First came the hurricane, then an earthquake and after that fire. God was not in any of them. God came later, in a small, quiet voice, or a 'brittle silence' as some newer translations have it. I like that. God is in the silence.

A much-related story in Hindu philosophy, which could just as well have been from the Buddhist practice, talks about a student who asks his teacher to explain Brahman, the soul of the world. Upon hearing the question, the teacher remains silent. The student repeats the question two or three more times, without receiving a single word in reply. Finally, the teacher opens his mouth and says: 'I am instructing you now, but you are not listening.'

The answer, of course, was silence.

Within Zen Buddhism, one goal is to challenge what you see, the visible world. The most well-known practice, a *koan*, is to sit quietly and imagine the sound of a single hand clapping. The point is to imagine the one-armed clapping – which is impossible – and to dwell on what it means to move beyond that which is logical and sensible. Another homemade *koan* that may be worthwhile imagining is this: silence without the existence of words. Or: try thinking about something that does not exist.

The ancient philosophers Aristotle and Plato spoke of the knowledge of eternity, and with it truth, as wordless. Plato called it *arrheton*, 'the unspeakable', and Aristotle *aneu logou*, which means 'without speech' or 'without words'. Where vocabulary ends, the two philosophers claimed, is an opening for the possibility of understanding great truths at once.

And not only the great truths, but the small ones too. For instance, when you end up driving in the wrong direction, are forced to stop, check the GPS, turn down the music and ask others in the car to quiet down so you can get some clarity in your head. This enables you to gather your thoughts about the one thing that holds any meaning in that one precise moment: finding the right direction.

《 》

17.

The starry sky 'is the truest friend in life, when you've first become acquainted; it is ever there, it gives ever peace, ever reminds you that your restlessness, your doubt, your pains are passing trivialities. The universe is and will remain unshaken. Our opinions, our struggles, our sufferings are not so important and unique, when all is said and done.' Most people who have spent a lot of time outside in the wild nod knowingly at the polar explorer Fridtjof Nansen's thoughts about things you may come to understand on a dark night.

And not only when you are outdoors, by the way. *The starry heavens above me and the moral laws within* are the two most important pillars highlighted by Immanuel Kant. Eyes cannot gaze at themselves, though you can study them via the stars: what you see in them depends on who you are.

As a Norwegian I'm privileged to be able to stare at the sky at night without the disturbance of man-made light. The stars are not visible if the light from street lamps comes between them and me. It's easy to forget that such a visual silence in large parts of the world is a rare thing. A luxury. That's also a pity. Being able to gaze out over a sky full of stars is one of the most rewarding things I know of. To be reminded of *the universe* that is above and far away from our own environment, and our own place in it.

Just before he died, the neurologist Oliver Sacks focused on starry nights. He wrote about how to exchange 'the hard problem' of understanding how the brain gives rise to consciousness and other ambitions for the benefit of merely sitting alone gazing at the stars. 'I saw the entire sky "powdered with stars" (in Milton's words); such a sky, I imagined, could be seen only on high, dry plateaus like that of Atacama in Chile (where some of the world's most powerful telescopes are). It was this celestial splendor that suddenly made me realize how little time, how little life, I had left. My sense of the heavens' beauty, of eternity, was inseparably mixed for me with a sense of transience – and death.' When he wrote this, Sacks was so weak that he could not walk and had to be pushed by friends in a wheelchair out to the night sky. Right at the end of his life, he began surrounding himself with metals and minerals as 'little emblems of eternity'. A practice he had not engaged in since childhood.

In knowing oneself, you know others. When I read Sacks, I feel that he, like Nansen, by turning his gaze upwards, also turned it inwards, towards his inner silence and uncovered forgotten sides. Into that universe which to me is just as mysterious as the outer space that surrounds us. One universe stretches outwards, the other inwards.

To me the latter universe is of the greatest interest. For, as the poet Emily Dickinson rightly concluded, 'The Brain – is wider than the Sky.'

《 》

18.

I like the idea that experiences of silence are an end unto themselves. Their value cannot be weighed and measured like so many other things, yet silence *can* also be a tool.

'Ha, ha, ha, ha, ha, ha,' was the reaction of the serial entrepreneur Elon Musk when I asked him about silence. But, after reflecting for a while, he concluded that he *is* someone who dwells on his own inner silence, often shutting out the world in order to open up his thoughts. Musk has been doing this his whole life. While growing up, he was often beaten up both in and outside school. With few friends at hand, he had time to think on his own.

When I talk to him about his yet-to-be realized ideas, it's clear he doesn't listen to consultants or other experts but rather to a quiet space inside himself. It's not enough for him to revolutionize the car, energy and aerospace industries. New disciplines must be turned on their heads. It is an ongoing revolution that will cease only when he's no longer

able to shut himself in with himself, but instead starts drifting with the current.

Musk is particularly good at using what is called *the first principle*: instead of relying on sanctioned truths, he uncovers what is fundamentally true in order to reason from that basis. He disconnects from the world. He does this in opposition to the normal way of operating: listening to what others say is possible, and building on that.

NASA scientists were always convinced that space shuttles could only be used once, which was a tremendously expensive accepted truth that had lingered since NASA's early days. This continued all the way up until the moment when Musk informed them that there was no reason not to build a shuttle that could be launched multiple times into space, and eventually to Mars. Costs would decrease, safety would increase.

I often find it hard to shut the world out when our days are so full. When I asked Mark Juncosa, one of the minds behind Musk's space programme, whether he ever has the chance to think out the ideas that could

revolutionize the rocket industry, he replied:
'A normal work day at best contains eight hours of
meetings, a few hours to respond to emails. It all blurs
together. The only time to shut out the world is when
I exercise, surf, take a shower or sit on the toilet.
That's when new solutions surface.'

I recognize this first principle in myself. I founded my
own company twenty years ago – a publishing house.
I was living in Cambridge, my girlfriend was pregnant,
she lived in Oslo, and I thought it was about time to
move back home, get a job and hopefully be able to
afford to buy a nice house for my family.

Back in Norway, as I was washing the dishes, I decided
to start a publishing house. The entire book industry
was dominated by an established truth that no one
had thought to question: books of high quality were to
be sold through booksellers and book clubs at a high
price. Romantic novels, on the other hand, were to
have the monopoly in supermarkets. Full stop. I didn't
understand why things had to be like that. Several
people offered me good advice. I'm grateful for that.

But thinking through the whole idea and taking a decision occurred while washing dishes, undisturbed, in the kitchen.

Another established truth is that you *must* be a big risk-taker if you wish to be an entrepreneur. This is a falsehood as well. I was constantly told that established authors would not want to have their books published by a start-up. They maintained that the literary culture was built into the walls of my competitors, who had been at it for a hundred years, and that it wasn't in our blood. I thought it was more important that the culture resided in the heads of my colleagues.

I am not so stupid as to compare myself to Elon Musk. However, when I look back on my time as a publisher, the only unusual thing I have done, on a completely different scale to Musk, was to stand uninterrupted at the kitchen sink and raise a few questions about sanctioned truths.

《 》

19.

'What we cannot speak about we must pass over in silence,' is the last sentence of Ludwig Wittgenstein's *Tractatus Logico-Philosophicus.* It is an artful formulation. The book was first rejected by his publisher, maybe because Wittgenstein claimed that the manuscript had two parts, the part that was written and a part that had not yet been written, and that the last part was the more important. Or perhaps because the publisher might have thought that it's precisely a philosopher who should be permitted to say that which others do not think speakable.

It was the chatter that Wittgenstein overheard in the decadent bourgeois salons of Vienna at the start of the 1900s which motivated him to draw such conclusions. Wittgenstein believed that the empty babble of his fellow countrymen threatened the very meaning of life. I tend to agree with him. It is frighteningly easy to dispose of time.

Tractatus was partly conceived in Skjolden, at the end of Lustrafjord, the innermost arm of the

Norwegian Sognefjord water inlet. Nature, silence and a distance from others shaped Wittgenstein and his philosophy: 'I cannot imagine that I could have worked in any other place as I have done here. It is the silence and, perhaps, the magnificent landscape; I mean its quiet gravity.'

The first time I heard his conclusions on staying quiet, I thought that Wittgenstein meant that we should relate passively to everything that we are unable to find words for. That seemed a bit clumsy. I found it difficult to understand that Wittgenstein could have reached such a conclusion from where he sat among the waterfalls, crags and valleys facing the fjord as he wrote. Of course, new horizons emerge beyond the unspoken. That is precisely *where* the fun begins. But I had misunderstood Wittgenstein. Which perhaps wasn't so strange, considering that just after buying *Tractatus* I had leafed through to the last page and read the final sentence.

I have since read everything that came before. And this is where Wittgenstein emphasizes that we can *show* what we are unable to find words for. 'What can be shown, cannot be said.' Words create boundaries: 'My whole tendency and, I believe, the tendency of all men who ever tried to write or talk Ethics or Religion was to run against the boundaries of language. This running against the walls of our cage is perfectly, absolutely hopeless.' By ethics, Wittgenstein means the very meaning of life. Not even science is able to find words for something like that. 'Ethics so far as it springs from the desire to say something about the ultimate meaning of the life, the absolute good, the absolute valuable, can be no science.' It must be shown, thought and felt.

20.

It feels good to share a joy.

On hectic days, I sometimes long for someone with whom I could do that. But this can also feel disruptive. In my late teens, I heard a story about the war hero Claus Helberg, who later became a respected guide in Norway's mountain region. The story seems like a random but precise response to Wittgenstein's idea about how, as long as you don't attempt 'to speak the unspeakable, *nothing* is lost'.

Early one morning, Helberg led a group of hikers out from Finsehytta, a famed Norwegian mountain cabin. The summer light was returning, winter had released its hold, and new colours were emerging everywhere. The conditions were fantastic, and instead of commenting on it he began the hike by handing out slips of paper to each of the participants on which was written: '*Yes, it is totally amazing.*'

Wittgenstein only partly followed his own ban on speaking about that which is unspeakable. He was not silent on the subject of remaining silent, but often talked about it. Helberg went further than Wittgenstein. He simply fell silent.

I've often thought of that story. After a long life on the mountain, and with an expansive understanding of occupying German forces, Helberg understood the way that words create boundaries for our experiences. He wanted to avoid a situation in which members of his group were continuously remarking to each other throughout the day on just how 'amazing' everything was, instead of actually concentrating on it being amazing.

Words can destroy the atmosphere. They are unsatisfactory. Yes, it is incredible to share grand experiences with others, but talking about it may distance us from what is happening. At times I am struck that it is the simple pleasures – such as studying green moss on a stone – which are the most difficult to put into words. Helberg wanted everyone to see, think and wonder at the mountains, the sky, and the moss and plants that had tentatively begun blooming for one more spring.

《 》

21

Is it possible to both be present in the world and not present at the same time? I think it is.

To me, those brief moments when I dwell on the horizon and am captivated by my surroundings, or when I do nothing more than study a rock with green moss and find myself unable to pull my eyes away, or else when I simply hold a child in my arms, are the greatest.

Time suddenly stops and I am simultaneously inwardly present and completely distant. All at once, a brief moment can seem like an eternity.

It is as if the moment and eternity become one. I have, of course, learned that they are opposites. Each on either end of the scale. But at times I am unable, as was the poet William Blake, to distinguish between eternity and that brief speck of time:

> *To see a World in a Grain of Sand*
> *And a Heaven in a Wild Flower,*
> *Hold Infinity in the palm of your hand*
> *And Eternity in an hour.*

I live for experiences like this. I feel like a pearl diver who, upon opening a shell, suddenly finds the perfect pearl.

Eternity, the moment or experience of having found the pearl, 'absolutely does not exist in time', writes the philosopher Søren Kierkegaard. In general, time is an 'endless Succession', where one second leads to the next. But suddenly the experience of time is changed, as succession is no longer endless after all. One second no longer leads to the next. Time is halted, and the present is no longer in opposition to past and future in the 'annulled Succession', as Kierkegaard formulated it. You experience the fullness of time in the moment.

The pleasure that I get in reading, feeling and thinking in these moments lies in the fact that they reflect the experiences that I have in nature, in bed, and when I read, experiences which I thought were far more unique when I was younger. Yet it turns out that these were not so unusual after all. The world is shut out for a moment, and an inner peace and silence takes over. These are feelings that I believe we all have

Ed Ruscha
Light Streak, 2003

to various degrees, in various ways, and which I think are worthwhile nurturing. Now and then I bring a mossy stone down from the mountain and place it on the kitchen counter or in the living room to remind myself about such experiences. Those stones of particular beauty I have given away as gifts. I always keep a stone sitting out at the office.

22.

'To compose poetry is about listening,' says Jon Fosse, '... not to contrive, it is, so to speak, about bringing forth something that already exists – this is why when one reads great poetry, one often gets this "I-knew-all-of-this-already, I-just-didn't-express-it feeling".' Fosse is influenced by his surroundings in Vestlandet, western Norway. If you listen, there is something being said to you, and that is what you write down. 'Language listens to itself.' Everything that doesn't come from within is in a way secondary information, according to my understanding of Jon Fosse. What comes to you externally has already been told. That which is vital, which is unique, is already within you.

One condition is that you must 'pull yourself back to a peace within yourself'. Jon Fosse does this when he is in western Norway, in Oslo or in a village outside Vienna. Life becomes more exciting when emotions are given more space to play. I feel, and then I think, therefore I am. Because, in addition to our habits, which of course impose multiple restraints, we are guided and driven by our feelings. It's easy to forget this at times, and so it can be helpful to reflect on the thoughts of people such as Nansen, Helberg and Fosse.

23.

That which is soundless within you remains a mystery. I don't think you should expect otherwise.

Even if all other great scientific puzzles were solved, I believe this one mystery would still remain. Science runs out of words and numbers. Silence is never old under the sun, it is new every time. Science is about observation over time, something that can be proven. Science explains material matter, what has been made. Or, better put, that which has been made which we are able to recognize and observe. But it is away from this recognition that silence begins.

As Fosse concludes, 'one may very well believe that only created matter exists, only the material. In that case, neither poetry nor philosophy nor Bach's music exist.' It would not only be poetry, philosophy and Bach that would cease to exist. Fosse is also thinking about you and me.

Keep in mind that the silence you experience is different from that which others experience. Everyone possesses their own.

« »

24.

It's common in music to have an absence of sound. It is an adventure listening to the compositions of Ludwig van Beethoven . . . da, da, da, daa . . . but it is the *cesur*, the pauses between the notes – the silence between the noises of the instruments – which are my favourite. That's when I am stirred awake.

Science has shown that such intervals are what generate the intense, positive neural activity that we experience. That is my experience as well. It's not only the notes. It is Beethoven's sudden silences that stir the mind and create a spark in your head. He understood that when we are exposed to silence, our minds and thoughts expand outwards. Miles Davis, the trumpet player and poet of loneliness, understood this too. In a musical genre full of festivity and extroversion, Davis became respected for the dramatic silences in his performances: the notes he chose not to play were as meaningful as those he did. At the end of his concerts, when the music ended, there was a sudden moment of silence before the applause. It felt as if your brain shifted gears.

Beethoven, as is well known, eventually went completely deaf. This development liberated a deep originality within him and a spirit of freedom. He composed his Ninth Symphony using the sounds existing solely within his head. During the premiere of the piece, he stood with his back to the audience in order to conduct the orchestra. After the music was over, he had to turn around to see whether the audience was clapping or booing. Not only were they clapping, their enthusiasm and cheers were so overwhelming that the Vienna police had to be called to restore peace and order.

Late in his life, Beethoven composed works that were too advanced for the audiences attending his concerts. Beethoven's pieces for string quartet were so modern that his contemporaries believed the music must be the result of an old man's madness. A hundred years later, when they were listened to again, the Beethoven quartets were hailed as masterpieces.

The composer John Cage, in his 'Lecture on

Nothing', which has been an inspiration to me, cited the composer Claude Debussy on his method of composing: 'I take all the tones there are, leave out the ones I don't want, and use all the others.' After that, Cage removed all of the tones in his piece *4' 33"* and created his silence for four minutes and thirty-three seconds. Audiences adore this piece of silence even today. Or rather: the silence minus the noises that the audience makes as they try to stay quiet.

Cage had many deep intellectual thoughts about silence; it's worthwhile listening to him on YouTube. But I tend to think about silence as a practical method for uncovering answers to the intriguing puzzle that is yourself, and for helping to gain new perspective on whatever is hiding beyond the horizon.

You can also listen through your jaw. After the inventor Thomas Edison, who was also deaf, came up with the phonograph, the predecessor to the record player, he had to lean over the player and bite hard into the woodwork that comprised the edge of the apparatus. That way he was able to feel the vibrations through his jaws. 'I bite my teeth in the wood good and hard and then I get it good and strong,' he said. As well as being his sole method of feeling his own invention, it was the only way he could enjoy the music.

25.

Contemporary music producers and artists have been criticized for piling sound effects on to every tune, never taking a chance on quieter moments, but I think the critics misunderstand a few things.

Of course, a lot of silence goes missing from old hits whenever they are remastered for MP3s, and because everyone now listens to music on earphones the soundscape is compromised and comes across as flatter. This is one of the reasons that vinyl sounds different. It is more *dynamic*; there are variations in volume.

However, silence still exists in music, even in newer recordings. It has simply become slightly higher over the years. When a hit such as 'Diamonds' by Rihanna was created, the producers began with silence. Well, they always begin with silence, according to them. First silence, and then components are painstakingly added. This first element, however, is the most important and also the most difficult. If too many instruments, ideas and noises are layered in it is hard to make the song work. They held back with 'Diamonds', and the melody is a fine example of how using fewer elements allows the original ideas to emerge with greater clarity.

A lot of silence can be found in the intros of contemporary pop songs, which have longer build-ups than they used to, before the arrival of what is known as *the drop*. That's the moment when the drums and the song's most important themes kick in. 'We're like diamonds in the sky.' Then things turn quiet again and the cycle repeats.

It's just as elsewhere in life: to get an important point across, it's wise to introduce a pause before and after the crux. Our brains prefer contrasts. They become attentive whenever the soundscape changes, and doze off when it remains monotone.

If you listen to DJs in an arena you'll hear one to three hours of build-up and drop, build-up and drop. When they increase the volume, use the dynamics, and the high pitches collide with my body, I am reminded that sound is something physical, something that moves through the air and can cause the venue to shake. Sound is air in motion. To bring out the bass, loudspeakers require a large surface area – there is a lot of air that has to be moved – while higher sounds require less surface area.

The DJ may insert a beat or two of silence before the drop. This silence creates anticipation, a sense that something is about to happen. Or alternatively, he or she might play a blast of high-frequency sound. The essential thing is the contrast between a little and a lot. It works every time. Your brain is eager to tune in when the music is in a borderland where it can fluctuate – suddenly it's quiet, a sound follows a soundless pause, or else you dance and wait for the tone to shift or the volume to change. It feels like your brain is expanding outwards. I am surprised at the reflections and thoughts that suddenly arise in those moments. On the other hand, if the soundscape remains steady and predictable then neural activity calms down: the brain is not being put to the test.

« »

26

High-pitched noises can have many modes of
expression, but the most powerful scream that I
have ever experienced is one that is void of sound: *The
Scream* by Edvard Munch. I fell silent upon looking at
it. There passed a communicative silence between the
painting and me. Yes, I know that I cannot hop into
the painting and be the person who lays a hand on the
screamer's right shoulder, yet I feel just as strongly
connected to the experience of the screamer.

The philosopher Denis Diderot believed that one
who observes interesting art is like a deaf man watching
mute signs on a subject known to him. The
formulation is a bit cumbersome, but it's accurate.
You *are* deaf when you stand there, attempting to
interpret what is placed, hung or presented before
you. The strange thing is that such a supposition also
applies to Marc Rothko's far more introspective
paintings. His large, rectangular fields of colour in
bold, often dark, hues are in a way the opposite of *The
Scream*. They seem to house an enormous battery of

Ed Ruscha
Double Light Streak, 2005

energy. 'Silence is so accurate,' said Rothko, when he refused to explain his images. Had he been able to simply reply with words, then perhaps he would have written an article instead of making a painting.

I am not sure why, but the fact is that a hush descends whenever you examine great art, trying to understand what the artist wanted to convey. It reminds me somewhat of Nansen's starry heavens.

A good work of art is like a *thinking machine* that reflects that artist's ideas, hopes, moods, failures and intuitions. Maybe I stay silent in front of art because I feel that I am separated from something every single day. There's so much I don't understand, that I can't move beyond, and art reminds me of that. I become more honest, more alive in what I am doing, and able to shut the world out. If, on top of that, I add a bit of goodwill, I can experience some of that feeling I have when I am exhausted on a long ski trip, or when I eat or drink something really delicious. Then I can no longer separate myself from what I am doing.

« »

27.

The performance artist Marina Abramović has made silence into an art form. Fosse leaves much of what he writes to silence, while Abramović in certain works is simply silent. She uses silence the way a musician uses sound or a painter the canvas.

In 2010 she sat for 736 hours and thirty minutes inside MoMA in New York, looking straight into 1,545 visitors' eyes without saying a word. The work was entitled *The Artist is Present*.

During the first days that Abramović sat in MoMA, she heard the same noises that we all hear inside a packed museum. People walking, milling about, speaking in hushed tones. After a few days she was able to perceive the cars passing outside the building. A few weeks later she heard the bumps from cars driving over one particular manhole cover in the street. I have never heard any noises other than those made by the public in MoMA, but I recognize the way in which basic senses are heightened during extended ventures into the wilderness. Or whenever I merely shut my eyes. My sense of smell and hearing improve. And if I cover my ears, I can see better.

According to Abramović, the opposite of silence is a brain at work. Thinking. If you wish to find peace, you must cease thinking. Do nothing. Silence is a tool helping us to escape the surrounding world. If you manage it, it becomes like 'a waterfall in your brain', she says. The electricity in the air changes when the world is shut out. It may last for a long time, or only for a mere fraction of a second. Time stands still, as Søren Kierkegaard discovered.

This concept sounds so simple, but it isn't. The first time Abramović travelled to the desert, she was afraid. She experienced the opposite of silence, although her surroundings were so quiet that the only thing she heard was the rush of her own blood as her heart pumped it through her body.

I have searched for absolute silence, but never found it. One of my friends made a serious attempt and locked himself into a soundproof room. The room was not only supposed to shut noises in, but it was also impossible to hear any noises from outside. The room was soundless. Or was it? My friend heard sounds inside too. Maybe he imagined them, or maybe it was the blood circulating around his body. I don't know, but I believe that absolute silence exists more as a dream than in reality.

Chaos. That is the word that Abramović uses when describing what she experienced in the desert. Despite the fact that everything was completely quiet around her, her head was flooded with disconnected thoughts. She struggled to find calm, even in the midst of silence. Her memories and thoughts jostled for her attention. It seemed like an *empty* emptiness, while the goal is to experience a *full* emptiness, she says. The empty emptiness was so uncomfortable that she is moved to this day whenever she speaks of it.

I recognize that experience. My head is flooded with pent-up thoughts and I am unable to shut out the world. The present must be *experienced*. That is what Abramović attempted to do, but her thoughts were about the past and the future. They were obstacles she had to go around. Creating silence is at times a minute act. I sometimes do it by jotting down my scattered thoughts on a piece of paper in order to empty my head of them. Afterwards I can take a look at my notes to see whether there was anything of interest that I should follow up on or simply remember. Abramović says that she tries to empty her head by breathing calmly through her nose, thereby gaining control over her breath. It is 'all about breathing'. This enables her to reach *her* goal, a full emptiness, a 'stillness of the mind'.

(A few weeks after this book was published in Norway I happened to meet Abramović. We talked about silence and she said the best way to describe it would be to put a blank sheet of A4 paper in a Xerox machine, and then hold the original and the copy next to each other. 'That is silence.')

《 》

28.

One poem that I have learned by heart is a haiku –
brevity's poetic form – by the Japanese poet Bashō:

An old pond.
A frog jumps in.
The sound of water!

When I recite it to myself, I picture calm
surroundings, the frog almost silently reaching the
water, and the tiny ripples in the otherwise glassy
surface spreading outwards in a circle where the frog
has landed.

Another Japanese poem written by an unknown
poet from the Matsushima group of islands is
comprised of only two words: 'O Matsushima'. I am
particularly fond of that poem. The poet was
apparently so overwhelmed by what he observed, the
beauty that revealed itself, that all he could manage
was to say the name of the islands before falling into
silence. Where the truth or reality don't permit

themselves to be put into words, as Wittgenstein and Helberg claimed, chatter seems to diminish. If the poet had continued writing more about the feelings he experienced, reflecting on them and conceptualizing, I fear his thoughts would have ruined the poem. The arrow leaves the bow, as a Zen master described the start of a bad poem, but 'does not fly straight to the target, nor does the target stand where it is . . .', and the poet fumbles his way around through too many words.

That which seems to take place between two people is naturally only a small part of the story. Below the surface something else is at play. If these vibrations were to be recorded, I suspect there would be enough noise for a Serbian brass band. I often recognize that something is going on, but I seldom understand it well.

When I travel in Japan, I feel this understanding rising to the surface. I don't know the language but I have the good fortune to be with people who have mastered it. For while we Norwegians experience silence in a conversation as something that cuts it off – a good journalist knows that the best moments in an interview often come just after they have put away their laptop or voice recorder and officially ended the interview – silence in Japan comprises a significant portion of the conversation. When I am able to observe two people speaking Japanese for a prolonged period, I am struck by how the short and long pauses feel as difficult to express as finding the right words. The silence seems to be just as rich in its content as the words.

The pauses seem like a bridge, with the two people having the conversation on opposite banks of the river, and when they speak again, they cross the river.

It is gaining mastery over silence for the sake of silence.

《 》

29

As a partner, I sometimes yearn for silence. I like to talk, and to listen, but it has been my experience that real intimacy is achieved when we don't speak for some time. Without the tenderness that can follow peace and quiet, it is difficult to sense the nuances in a loving relationship, to understand one another. Chatter and other noises can easily become defence mechanisms to help avoid the truth. Yes, when everything I want is in my arms, words are superfluous. Depeche Mode sang:

> *All I ever wanted*
> *All I ever needed*
> *Is here in my arms*

That's when words can harm, the band goes on to sing in their synthrock anthem. There is, as Stendhal claimed in *On Love*, always an element of doubt in a successful relationship. This doubt 'endows each moment with desire, this is what gives life the successful love'. Where fear is ever present you will never tire of pleasure in the relationship. It sounds brutal, but Stendhal is right. Life is brutal. I am living dangerously when I take a relationship for granted. Most people think climbing Everest is very risky, but things usually work out. However, taking reciprocal love for granted – I would never dare do that.

This form of success is characterized by its seriousness, says Stendhal. For me, it's when we are able to sit together in silence.

Talking and listening to music can open doors, but it can also shut the same doors to what is essential. If your partner doesn't understand you when you are silent, mightn't it be even harder for them to understand you when you're speaking? I believe so. In any case, poets, authors and musicians have for the most part already expressed the words that are natural to say to someone you are in love with, so the chances that your beloved has already heard your well-formulated words – perhaps even in a better form – are pretty high. As the mystic Rumi is said to have written: 'Now I shall be silent, and let the silence divide that which is true from that which lies.'

« »

30.

More than twenty years ago, a psychologist, Arthur Aron, was able to get complete strangers to fall in love in his laboratory. Two people meet: they don't know each other, but based on a questionnaire filled out beforehand they have several things in common. During the experiment, the paired-up participants are then asked a series of thirty-six questions such as: 'Given the choice of anyone in the world, whom would you want as your dinner guest?' (question no. 1); 'Take turns sharing something you consider a positive characteristic of your partner, a total of five items' (no. 17) – it's important here to choose your words carefully; and 'What is your most treasured memory?' (no. 28).

Question no. 36 is . . . Well, I'd suggest you look that up yourself.

After Aron's questions, the experiment ends with both participants sitting and looking into each other's eyes without saying a word for up to four minutes.

Two of these subjects got married six months later and invited everyone from the laboratory to the wedding.

One of the most widely read articles in *The New York Times* in 2015 was by the journalist Mandy Len Catron, who tried out Aron's theories in practice. She acknowledged in the end that falling in love isn't something that merely happens, it is an act, and she chose a variety of fine clichés to describe those four silent minutes of nothing but eye contact:

I've skied steep slopes and hung from a rock face by a short length of rope, but staring into someone's eyes for four silent minutes was one of the more thrilling and terrifying experiences of my life. I spent the first couple of minutes just trying to breathe properly. There was a lot of nervous smiling until, eventually, we settled in.

I know the eyes are the windows to the soul or whatever, but the real crux of the moment was not just that I was really seeing someone, but that I was seeing someone really seeing me. Once I embraced the terror of this realization and gave it time to subside, I arrived somewhere unexpected.

The questions are clever. I have tried this experiment myself. It's almost hypnotic. The other listens, you feel that you are understood, they look at and respect you without further introduction. When you are finally finished gazing into their eyes – by the way, four minutes seems like a very long time – it is as though you are being pulled towards each other.

31.

I have never been quick to learn. I was so dyslexic as a young boy that I wasn't even able to pronounce the word *dyslexic* until I turned twenty. The experiences that I was able to absorb – while far away on the ice in Antarctica, beneath Manhattan, hiking around Oslo, on my way to the office, or back at home in my chair – were the pleasures taken from small things. Gratitude for food when I am famished following a long day. Listening to and seeing the nuances that I normally don't recognize. Uncovering new thoughts and ideas in the space between my two ears. Catching small fish. Taking small bites.

Allow the world to vanish when you go into it.

To listen is to search for new opportunities, to seek fresh challenges. The most important book you can read is the one about yourself. It is open. I've started to understand why I was so fascinated as a small boy by the snail who carries his house on his back. We can also carry our houses – everything that we have – within us.

Now and then someone asks me what the most difficult thing about skiing through Antarctica was, and there is no doubt in my mind about the answer: my arrival at the South Pole. Having to speak again. The first words I heard when I reached my destination were: 'How do you do?'

I had been wearing the same underwear for the previous fifty days and nights, and so replied: 'Like a pig in shit.' It was more difficult to start talking again than it had been to get up early all of those fifty mornings. Being on the journey is almost always more satisfying than reaching the goal. We prefer the hunt for the rabbit over its capture.

《 》

Most of the people I meet have enough knowledge to fill nine lives. There has never been a book written that can tell you more than what *you* yourself have experienced.

So, take a deep breath. Not much is required to understand silence and how you can take pleasure in shutting out the world. This bit of knowledge, as the poet Olav H. Hauge writes, is something which your heart has always possessed:

> *When it comes to the punch, there's*
> *so little left to do, and that tiny bit*
> *the heart has always known.*

Which paths lead to silence? Certainly trips into the wild. Leave your electronics at home, take off in one direction until there's nothing around you. Be alone for three days. Don't talk to anyone. Gradually you will rediscover other sides of yourself.

*

The most important thing, however, is not what I believe, but that we each discover our own way. You, my own three daughters, me – all of us have our own paths. *Sva marga*: follow your own path. It is easier to find silence than many people think or believe. And neither professors, psychologists, Pascal, Cage nor a father of three like me are able to fully explain everything in words. It feels good to wonder on your own. Fortunately, there's no magic spell.

I had to use my legs to go far away in order to discover this, but I now know it is possible to reach silence anywhere. One only need subtract.

You have to find your own South Pole.

33.

Notes

The various quotations and sources referenced in this book are drawn from a wide range of places: expeditions, family, events I have attended, and people and ideas I have met, read or heard about. This is an attempt at listing those sources I can easily recall.

Introduction

The speech referred to in the introduction was organized by TEDx at St Andrews, 26 April 2015. 'Another Lecture on Nothing' is the title.

1

Jon Fosse's quotes in answer 1 are taken from emails between him and myself. His quotes in answers 22 and 23 are from *Mysteriet i trua* (The mystery of faith), a conversation between Fosse and Eskil Skjeldal (Samlaget, 2015).

2.

The principal Martin Heidegger references
are from *Sein und Zeit* (*Being and Time*; 1927).
Additional references (as in answer 15) are from his
speech on technology, 'The Question Concerning
Technology', given in 1953, as well as from various
articles on the internet. And just to be clear: I have
not read *Sein und Zeit* in its entirety.

6.

The Silence That Follows was written by Rolf
Jacobsen and first published in *Stillheten etterpå*,
Dikt (Glydenal, Denmark, 1965). I don't think it has
ever been published in English.

7.

The somewhat dubious study of goldfish is widely documented. I mainly relied on this article: http://time.com/3858309/attention-spans-goldfish.

David Foster Wallace's note originates here: http://www.vulture.com/2009/03/will_david_foster_wallace.html. This was discovered together with the manuscript of his last book, *The Pale King* (Little, Brown, 2011).

The Blaise Pascal quotation, and the references to what he wrote, are taken from his 1669 *Pensées* (*Thoughts*). I read a Norwegian translation (PAX, 2007).

8.

The research referred to in answer 8 has been widely discussed and written about. I have in particular relied on this article for my book: www.eurekalert.org/pub_releases/2014-07/uov-dsi063014.php.

I also had the pleasure of reading *Back to Sanity* by Steve Taylor (Hay House, 2012), as well as an article written by Oliver Burkeman in the *Guardian*, 20 July 2014: http://www.theguardian.com/lifeandstyle/2014/jul/19/change-your-life-sit-down-and-think.

9.

In reference to Twitter and its founders as they
begin to second-guess their creation, these
reflections arose during a conversation I had
with one of Twitter's founders, Evan Williams,
just outside London in the autumn of 2015.

The reference to the *New York Review of Books* is
for an article by Jacob Weisberg, 'We are Hopelessly
Hooked', from 25 February 2016.

I mention two sailing trips across the Atlantic.
Hauk Wahl, Arne Saugstad and Morten Stødle
(the latter only heading west) were the other
crew members.

10.

The quote about 'those days that came and went'
is from the Swedish poet Stig Johansson.

The Seneca the Younger quote is from '*De
Brevitate Vitae*' ('On the Shortness of Life').

12.

The account of Lars Fr. H. Svendsen's thoughts on boredom are from his classic *The Philosophy of Boredom* (*Kjedsomhetens filosofi;* Universitetsforlaget, 1999), as well as from conversations with him during the writing of this book.

The phrase *experiential poverty*, to the best of my knowledge, was first used by the relatively unknown German philosopher Martin Doehlemann. His words for it were *Erlebnisarmut* and *Erfahrungsarmut*.

13.

I read about the birdsong in the book *One Square Inch of Silence: One Man's Quest to Preserve Quiet* by Gordon Hempton and John Grossman (Atria Books, 2010), which again refers to the *New Scientist* (December 2006), as well as *Molecular Ecology*'s article 'Birdsong and Anthropogenic Noise: Implications and Applications for Conservation'.

14.

The soundproofed hall mentioned is Vækstcenteret
(The Centre for Growth) in Denmark. I've not been
there myself, but have read multiple accounts of it,
including in the Danish newspaper *Politiken*: http://
politiken.dk/magasinet/feature/ece2881825/tag-en-
pause-med-peter-hoeeg/. (This article is in Danish.)

There were three of us who walked across LA
together: Peder Lund, Petter Skavlan and myself.

17.

Oliver Sacks's essay 'My Periodic Table', which I
mention in answer 17, has been published by numerous
outlets. I first read it in *Gratitude* (Picador, 2015).

18.

The quotations and other materials relating to Elon
Musk and Mark Juncosa are from questions I asked
them partly in the context of this book, mostly
while in Los Angeles in the winter of early 2016.

19.

The first Ludwig Wittgenstein quotation is the
closing sentence of *Tractatus Logico-Philosophicus*.
The second quotation is from the same book,
section 4.1212. The quotation where he emphasizes
the beauty of working in Skjolden is from a letter
he wrote in 1936, which I found on Wikipedia.

The next quotation is from a collection of
articles: *Wittgenstein and the Philosophy of Religion*,
edited by Robert L. Arrington and Mark Addis
(Routledge, 2004).

The last quotation is from the book *Tracking
the Meaning of Life: A Philosophical Journey* by Yuval
Lurie (University of Missouri Press, 2006).

20.

The Wittgenstein quotation is from *Det stille alvoret*
(The quiet seriousness), edited by Knut
Olav Åmås and Rolf Larsen (Samlaget, 1994).

The anecdote about Claus Helberg was told to me
by the polar explorer Herman Mehren, who knew
Helberg well, and had heard it first hand from him.

21.

The Søren Kierkegaard quotations are taken
from Ettore Rocca's book *Kierkegaard* (Gyldendal,
Denmark, 2015).

25.

Tor Erik Hermansen, one of the two members of
the music production outfit Stargate, talked with
me about silence, music, Rihanna's 'Diamonds'
(which they produced), and other topics for
this book, in Oslo in the summer of 2016. Mekia
Machine and Kaja Nordengen offered further
information for answer 25.

26.

The phrase *thinking machine* in regards to a work
of art in answer 26 is good, but it's not mine. I have
picked it up somewhere or other.

27.

I was fortunate enough to be able to ask Marina
Abramović a few questions in the summer of 2016.
She was in Las Vegas, according to her 'the most
horrible place on earth', and I was in Oslo. Petter
Skavlan, who was in Las Vegas with Abramović,
conducted the interview as a favour, based on
questions we had both agreed on. Her responses
here are drawn from their conversation.
My friend who went into the soundproof room was
the composer Henrik Hellstenius.

28.

It has been claimed that Bashō wrote 'O Matsushima', but nobody seems to know for sure. Additionally it is not clear whether the poem has one or three lines:

> *Matsushima ah!*
> *A-ah, Matsushima, ah!*
> *Matsushima, ah!*

I am not the one to know which is the most accurate, but personally I prefer the short version with two words and one line.

The Zen master who describes the start of a bad poem is D. T. Suzuki.

29.

The quote by Stendhal in answer 29 is from the Norwegian version of *On Love: Om kjærlighet* (Gyldendal, 2005).

30.

The article about falling in love in thirty-six questions can be found here: http://www.nytimes.com/2015/01/11/fashion/modern-love-to-fall-in-love-with-anyone-do-this.html.

32.

The Olav H. Hauge poem '*Når det kjem til stykket*' was first published in *På Ørnetuva* (Oslo: Noregs Boklag, 1961).

Acknowledgements

I would like to express my thanks to Joakim Botten,
Kathrine Aspaas, Jon Fosse, Kristin B. Johansen, Liv
Gade, Gabi Gleichmann, Lars Fr. H. Svendsen, Morten
Faldaas, Iselin Shumba, Petter Skavlan, Ed Ruscha,
Nick Baylis, Haraldur Örn Ólafsson, Josefine Løchen,
Jan Kjærstad, Finn Skårderud, Doug Aitken, Erlend
Sørskaar, Lars Mytting, Knut Olav Åmås, M.M.,
Odd-Magnus Williamson, Tor Erik Hermansen,
Kaja Nordengen, Anne Britt Granaas, Bjørn Fredrik
Drangsholt, Aslak Nore, Mah-Rukh Ali, Mary Dean,
Suzanne Brøgger, Ellen Jervell, Leif Ove Andsnes,
Åsne Seierstad, Anne Gaathaug, Sindre Kartvedt,
Michelle Andrews, Becky L. Crook, Catherine Opie,
Marina Abramović, Mekia Machine, Mark Juncosa,
Elon Musk, Hanneline Røgeberg, Nick Baylis, Dan
Frank, Hans Petter Bakketeig, Joel Rickett, Sonny
Mehta, Annabel Merullo and everyone at J. M.
Stenersens Forlag and Kagge Forlag.

Images

VIKING

UK | USA | Canada | Ireland | Australia
India | New Zealand | South Africa

Viking is part of the Penguin Random House group of companies
whose addresses can be found at global.penguinrandomhouse.com.

First published in Norwegian as *Stillhet i støyens tid: Gleden*

ved å stenge verden ute by Kagge Forlag AS 2016
This translation first published by Viking 2017

001

Text design by Claire Mason
Typeset by Penguin Books
Printed in China by C&C offset Printing Co., LTD.

A CIP catalogue record for this book is available
from the British Library

ISBN: 978–0–241–30987–2

www.greenpenguin.co.uk

Catherine Opie
Sunset IV, 2009

Erling Kagge is an explorer who was the first in history to reach the 'three poles' – North, South and the summit of Everest. During these expeditions, he experienced extreme periods of silence – the longest being fifty days. He has since returned to Norway and searches for moments of silence among noisy family life and his work as a writer and publisher. *Silence* is an international best-seller and has been translated into thirty-three languages.